Funand Drills

#1 Best Seller on Amazon Kindle!

Written by: Steve Adler

Awarded Amazon's "Best Selling Author for Sports & Outdoors/Baseball"

All Rights Reserved. No part of this publication may be reproduced in any form or by any means, including scanning, photocopying, or otherwise without prior written permission of the copyright holder.

Copyright © 2014. First Edition 2014.

Published by SunVision Media

Printed in the United States of America
ISBN-13: 978-1499664409
ISBN-10: 1499664400

Learn more information or contact the author at his author page on Amazon.

AVAILABLE ON KINDLE DEVICES

From:

Date:

Table of Contents

Introduction 1

Chapter 1 – Playing Catch 3

Chapter 2 – The Fundamental Pitch Drills 13

Chapter 3 – Primary Balance Drill 19

Chapter 4 – The Curl Drill 24

Chapter 5 – The Heels Relations Drill 30

Chapter 6 – Dot the Eye Drill (Secondary Balance) . 35

Chapter 7 – The Count Drill 41

Chapter 8 – The Pitch Drill 54

In Summary 59

Glossary 61

Dedication

I dedicate this teaching manual to my wife Debbie who supported my enormous amount of time away from my family that it took to be a good coach. Also to my dad who introduced me to baseball and how to love it and think outside the box. And lastly to all my wonderful Lancers who for over 35 years believed in "Lancer Baseball" and played the game the way it is supposed to be played.

Introduction

Arguably, the most important position in the game of baseball is the pitcher. The pitcher controls the tempo of the game by how fast he works and his ability to throw strikes. Both keep the game flowing as well as keeping fielders alert and spectators interested. Those factors can influence the outcome of a game and make bearable the cold spring games played in the geographic region where I coach. I decided early on in my coaching career that if I was to last as a baseball coach in Michigan I better design a program that adapted to the weather. I wanted the games to be interesting and quick. One of the first things I did was adopt parts from other coaches and from watching the game closely my whole life. One of those was the motto of Ray Miller, Baltimore Oriole pitching coach from the 70"s. His simple motto which now almost 40 years of my own pitchers can quote is to:

- Work Fast
- Throw Strikes
- Change Speeds

I call these our Game Day Motto and preach to my players.

If you do these three things you have a great chance to be a success:

1. **If** you are fundamentally sound.
2. **If** you trust those fundamentals. And,
3. **If** you repeat those fundamentals over and over.

Umpires love to do our games because of the quick pace our pitchers worked and the ability to throw strike one and strike two on a consistent basis. Our players appreciated all the strikes being thrown as well. Fielders made routine plays and innings passed quickly because of pitchers throwing a great majority of strikes to balls. Games were not the long dragged out affair that they could have been because of this.

How do you get there? It's a mental and physical approach that takes years of hard work. It's a process. My players hear this from day one, over and over. **IT IS A PROCESS**. Time and effort, physical and mental, are necessary to learn this process. And it takes years. I motivate my pitchers by teaching them they **must be the best of the best** on our high school team if they want to have a chance to play college baseball. If you want to be the best of the best you have to put the time in to learn the physical and mental aspects that it takes and never stop working on this part of your game.

In this manual I'm going to teach the physical and mental aspects of pitching that I find the most important and can be a starting point for the very young and can take older players through the high school level of play. The lessons I will teach are:

1. How to properly play catch, including my statue drill so a pitcher is constantly working on his craft.
2. My six pitching drills

Future lesson manuals will deal with how to properly hold runners, arm strengthening and arm care during the off season, the preseason and in season. But let's get started on the process to become a pitcher who can throw strikes and move a game along while being a success.

Chapter 1
Playing Catch

To me, pitching begins when a player is merely playing catch with a dad or a teammate. It's possible to help all players understand that if they have the desire to pitch they need to first work on a few basic fundamentals every time they throw a ball. It should be and is easily stressed to even the youngest of players that the game of catch is very important. I stress that we are playing catch….. not chase. In a pregame situation it's the first chance to show the other team you mean business. Catch should always be purposeful and done in a correct manner. Other teams notice when a good game of catch is going on by the opponents and take note. "These guys are good." Just the way kids play catch sends this message.

Catch also gets those who will be your pitchers to constantly think about improving as a pitcher every chance they get. It must be stressed and players need to buy in to the idea that they are working on this part of their game seriously every time they throw……even if they aren't going to pitch that day. It's vital for all pitchers to constantly be thinking like a pitcher when they play catch to give the simplest game of catch purpose.

Whether its pre-practice or pregame we jog, stretch then throw. The coach should be right there and in control of when to back players up every few throws. A good coach will coach at this time not just allow kids to warm up on their own. Players should be throwing in game uniform only. I do not let them warm up in a jacket or hoodie. If the weather is cold jackets and hoodies are encouraged as soon as warm up is over.

After several minutes we back off and play proper long toss which I'll explain in a future manual when we talk about arm strengthening. We long toss about ten throws and close it back down to just beyond pitching mound distance. This is when all pitchers do the Statue Drill. With older boys I insert a Shuffle Change Up drill prior to the Statue Drill. When we play catch there are four main things that need to be stressed.

1. Squaring the back foot.
2. Pointing the shoulder at the target.
3. Thumbs point down on separation.
4. Hit our lines.

As a coach I am right there with them stressing these four points. I'll call out……..**"square that back foot"…………"point your shoulder"……….."thumbs down"……………"hit your lines."** I'm also in charge of moving them back as I walk along the side while they throw. I insist that if players can catch the ball in rhythm, to catch with two hands. Only on a bad throw do I allow one handed catches. This puts some structure in the simplest pregame activity. And it looks sharp when kids catch with two hands and throw in a uniform manner.

As I stated every time a pitcher throws a ball he should be working on his craft. It's with this in mind that I add a visual target to this activity. I tell them to imagine a triangle on their partner's chest with lines running from shoulder to shoulder then to the belly button. It is encouraged that players throw "bulls eyes" within that triangle. Again I chant encouragement as reminders……."**hit that bulls eye."** Now let's take a closer look at the four main coaching points to a game of catch as the beginning of becoming a pitcher.

Squaring the Back Foot

Illustration 1

As you can see in **Illustration 1** the back foot must be square every time a baseball is thrown. Proper technique is to have the player pick up his back foot and turn it 45 degrees so it is square like when he engages the rubber. The foot should not be dragged to this position. It must be picked up, turned and placed down. Allowing players to be lazy and drag the foot or not get it square every time will develop other throwing issues. Never allow a player to point his back foot at his target. In the process of learning to throw the back foot is the initial trigger. The back foot must be square to get all other points engaged properly. This strong back foot stance triggers everything else about throwing.

Pointing the Shoulder at the Target

The next two coaching points take place almost at the same time. But slowing the process down pointing the front shoulder closely follows the squaring of the back foot just before turning the thumbs downward. I like to stress that the ball goes where the shoulder points and its necessary to point the front shoulder as long as possible at the target. I tell my players to point until the front foot hits the ground. It's not always possible but it keeps their front shoulder closed and not pointing away from the target. In **Illustration 2** you will note that the player points his front shoulder at his target and looks directly over that shoulder.

Point the Thumbs Down On Separation

This is a trick I uses to help get the elbows up. I especially want the back elbow to be higher than the shoulder when the throw is released. By turning the thumbs down to face the ground both front and back elbow are forced up. In **Illustration 3** notice the thumbs pointing down and both elbows straight and high. Many players throw with a low throwing elbow. This causes the ball to sail up and in to the throw side arm. Position players should strive to throw with a high throw side elbow. An easy way to accomplish this is to stress and expect that players turn their thumbs down when they separate their hands after any catch.

Hit Our Lines

This is a pet peeve of mine. Players do one thing in a drill when you stand over them and repeat instructions to them but do another as soon as they are on their own. Players tend to get lazy in the game of catch when a coach isn't stressing the four main catch points. They need to be trained to do the same thing every time they throw. Hitting their lines seems to be the most difficult to do. To hit our lines we must first know what they are.

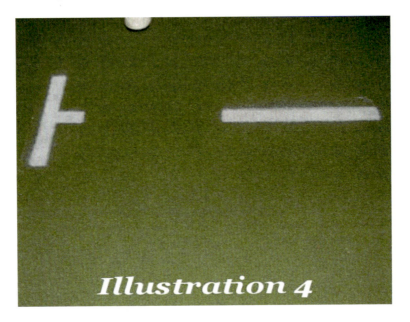

In the dirt it's easy to draw a reminder line from where the back foot is squared straight ahead. **(See Illustration 4)** Indoors tape can be used or paint.

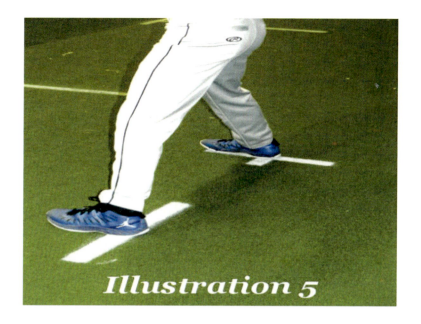

Illustration 5

Every time a throw is made the player needs to hit his line with his front foot. **(Illustration 5)**

Illustration 6

If the foot is too far to the left for a right handed thrower, it can cause flying open of the front shoulder and the ball may be yanked to the left. Remind the kids that the ball goes where the shoulder leads and the shoulder can follow the foot placement. **(See Illustration 6)**

The most general problem though, when not hitting the line, is throwing with the foot in a closed position. **(See Illustration 7)** This causes the front side of the body to fight the back side of the body and can eventually lead to a weary arm or sore arm and a gradual loss of velocity. Insist and point out each time a player doesn't hit his lines while playing catch.

Statue Drill

After your players are loose and have even played a little loss toss at your direction I alert all pitchers, "Statue Drill." Players who are not pitchers may jog to the dugout but all those who are pitchers regardless of whether they are going to pitch on that given day are required to throw an additional 8-10 throws in both parts of this drill. The Statue Drill is simply stressing to hold primary and secondary balance points for a full second before and after throwing. More about this drill after primary and secondary balance have been explained at the end of Chapter 6.

Summary

Whenever a baseball player needs to throw these four principals apply. Whether they are an infielder, outfielder or catcher they should square their back foot, point their front shoulder, turn their thumbs down when the hands separate and hit their lines whenever they make a throw. These are solid baseball fundamentals which when stressed will make kids a better defensive player and will give those who want to pitch a definite advantage.

Chapter 2
The Fundamental Pitch Drills

Remember learning to pitch is a process. It takes many years of dedication working on fundamentals to learn this important part of the game. It helps to have a good arm but fundamentals are more important and often those who have great basics become much better pitchers than those with the naturally strong arm. It's also possible to gain arm strength. I tell kids that they need to trust and repeat their fundamentals. Arm strength will catch up especially if they work on that aspect of pitching in the off season. There will be more about when and how to gain arm strength in future manuals. I have coached many kids with a great deal of determination apply and work on the drills I'm about to introduce become very successful high school pitchers. Many of these players went on to play college baseball.

The drills are the major part of the process of learning to pitch. They must be done over and over and more often than just in the presence of their coach. I encourage my pitching students to do them at least three times a week in the off season and to keep a journal to record when they did them. Keeping a journal also gives a player a great sense of accomplishment when they show it to their coach after a couple months.

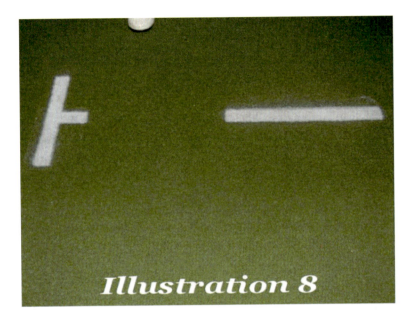

Illustration 8

It's a big help if the player has an area at home in the basement or garage where they put down a Pitch Tee. This is useful in all the drills, especially for hitting their lines. They can use tape or draw lines in the dirt for this purpose. **(See Illustration 8)** A Pitch Tee is an important tool in our process.

I have named the fundamental pitch drills:

- Primary Balance Drill
- The Curl Drill
- Heal Relations Drill
- Dot the Eye Drill (Secondary Balance)
- Count Drill
- Pitch Drill

I urgently stress to players the importance to be able to repeat parts of a learned drill in each following drill. The order of the drills follows the pitching process and therefore fundamentals of one drill leads into the next drill. Coaches need to stress and be aware for players to add on something new to the next drill while understanding fundamentals learned in the previous drill need to be maintained. Sometimes a coach will need to backtrack if players "cheat the drill" by not repeating fundamentals previously learned. Again it is a process and takes attention to detail if a coach wants his players to improve and if the player values becoming the best of the best. This attention to repeating fundamentals learned in a previous drill will assist the players in all sports they will play in the future. I ask my players to be coach-able and do not hesitate backtracking to repeat a drill if players are being lazy on parts being repeated in the next drill.

As stated earlier I repeat each drill four times and stress details between the repetitions. I use players as examples to others in a positive manner and use humor to prod those who need improvement. Constant motivation to believe in the drills and believe they can become the best of the best is used throughout the lesson. It might be necessary to remind players that learning to pitch is a process and most of that process is spent on fundamentals. The six coach led drills repeated four times each takes about half the hour lesson. The second part of the lesson is used to work on holding runners using proper mechanics to shorten delivery in order to contain the running game of your opponent. Again it should be coach led to assure players are doing it properly. Once we have gone through the drills and worked on holding runners players are given several minutes to play catch. Constant reminder about the fundamentals of catch might be necessary. Older players end with the Statue Drill before we go to the mounds to throw for the final twelve minutes or so of the lesson. The closer we get to the season the shorter we do the fundamental drills and the longer we spend pitching to a catcher. When throwing to a catcher I have players throw three pitches at a time and rotate. I also stretch this out as we condition the arm closer to the approaching season.

The rotation I use for throwing to a catcher in the preseason is as follows. Throw in sets of three until we get closer to the season and I add pitches to the rotation. This is an integral part of conditioning the arm for the season. I do however limit the number of pitches in a given rotation just before the season begins to fifteen at a time to try and simulate an innings work. That would be fifteen pitches and fifteen off while the next student throws as if their team were hitting. I always direct what we are throwing and if we are holding runners or not. When in the three pitch rotation I have pitches throw the first three out of the windup, the next set of three they are holding a man on first and the next set holding a man on second. This may be the only nine pitches they throw total in the early preseason. During subsequent sessions they may throw four or five pitches in each rotation leading up to the fifteen just prior to the season. As for breaking pitches and change ups as the sessions of throw rotations are extended I will have them throw a cut fastball for older kids one week and the change ups the next week. Again three pitches at a time as many rotations as time left in the lesson allows. For kids younger than thirteen I only teach the change up and use it the same way as add on rotations to the end of lessons after kids have used the windup, first base and second base holds.

To summarize what an hour weekly preseason lesson looks like:

- Pre lesson motivation and POE (Point of Emphasis) for the day
- Fundamental Drills
- Holding Runners
- Warm up stretch and throw
- Statue Drill (older pitchers)
- Rotation Pitches

First few weeks:

- Use last ten or twelve minutes of the session.
- Three pitches and rotate. Have pitchers throw only fastballs.
- First rotation throws three pitches out of the wind up.
- Second rotation throws holding a runner on first.
- Next rotation throws holding a runner on second. Additional pitches can be added to time allotted, but I don't exceed the ten or twelve minutes.

Middle four weeks:

- Use last 15 minutes of the session and add a few pitches to each rotation. Allow older players to work on a secondary pitch with several of their throws. One week work on the change up, the next week work on the cut fastball. Continue the wind up and holding runner sequence.

Last few weeks:

- Using the final twenty to twenty five minutes of the session pitchers will be throwing fifteen pitches in each rotation and mix holds and secondary pitches more often at coach's discretion. I limit each pitcher to two rotations as stated above. It's necessary to use two catchers so all four pitchers (the usual size) in the group get their fifteen pitches two times. This along with regularly catching in the preseason also helps get the catcher's get ready for the season not only catching all pitchers but gives them a chance to condition their legs and work on framing pitches. I ask them to catch three pitches as they would in a game given the pitcher is winding up or in the stretch. They are told they can "Cadillac" the next three pitches.

Final note: In the preseason, I motivate the players to continue to work on arm strengthening using floor exercises and 10-12oz heavy balls when doing their at home fundamental drills. I stress that we never throw a heavy ball and if players are multi-sport athletes who lift weights, lots of stretching is necessary to avoid bulking and not have a loose arm to pitch. I will review much this all in more detail in the next manual. And a note about POE. I like to give players a Point of Emphasis for every practice and pitchers doing lessons are no different. I pick a fundamental that I think is lacking or just select a specific fundamental that we stress more than others on that day. Example: "Today's POE is balance over the rubber." In drills and rotation pitching I now will stress balance over the rubber more than normal. This allows a coach to work all the drills weekly with a specific emphasis on a given fundamental. After several weeks, several POE's have given us additional work on a fundamental area. Okay,

On to the drills...

Chapter 3
Primary Balance Drill

"Ready, Ready" is the command I give before each and every drill repetition. I call this the trigger for my players. This way no matter what I'm about to teach players know I want them in the ready position. For pitchers prior to each repetition the ready position is what I call the Prayer Position. **(Illustration 9)**

"Ready, Ready" puts all pitches in the group in the same starting point and get them focused to begin their work.

I tell all pitching prospects from the very youngest I teach that if you want to be a pitcher you have to have balance. You can't pitch unless you have balance………..more specifically balance over the rubber. This is one of the most common problems that pitchers young and old have no balance over the rubber. When a coach notices a pitcher throwing ball one and ball two to batters consistently it is very probable that balance is missing. We begin every pitching lesson with the Primary Balance Drill.

Start with the player standing square on his Tee.

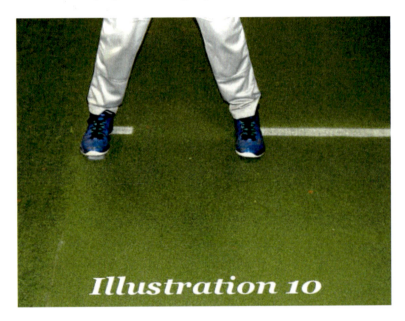

This is an exact repetition of squaring his back foot when playing catch. Feet are shoulder width apart. **(Illustration 10)**

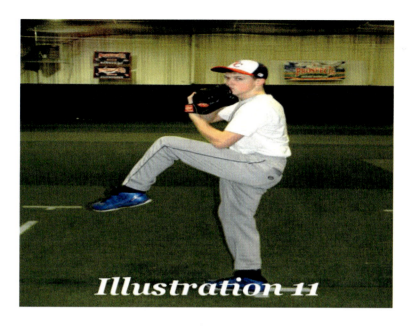

Illustration 11

When given the command from the coach.........**"Ready, Ready."** Then....... **"Ready.......Up"** the player raises his left leg (right hand pitchers) to reach at least the level of his belly button. **(Illustration 11)** Hands are in the middle of the chest **(Illustration 11)**. The coach counts aloud......**"thousand one, thousand two, thousand three.......down."** The player tries to hold his balance with a flat back. **(Illustration 11)** Repeat the drill four times stressing knee up to the belly button and a flat, straight back. Again, the player needs to be constantly reminded that this is the beginning of the process and most necessary to achieve if they want to consistently throw strikes. Another coaching point I make in this drill is to stress that the left leg is not only belly button or higher but is spread away from their plant leg **(Illustration 11).**

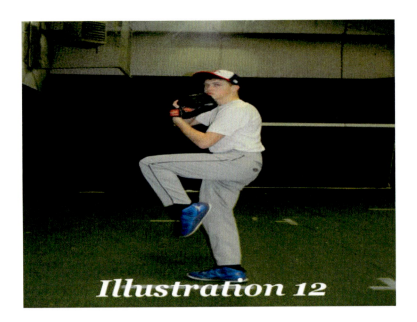

I like to have fun with my players so I tell them if their front leg is bent close to their plant leg they look like a Flamingo. **(Illustration 12)** I tell them we don't want to be a Flamingo because as late night talk show host Craig Ferguson likes to tease, Flamingos pee on themselves to stay cool. It gets a chuckle every time and helps make the session fun. This is also where I instruct players to point their front toe down to the ground. **(Illustration 11)**

I tell them to look pretty. **"Pitchers should look pretty."** Also gets a chuckle. Lots of pitchers starting out doing this drill will arch their back. It's necessary that the back remains straight **(Illustration 11)**. Younger pitchers can be told to lower their raised leg and gradually increase its height if it means having a straight back. When done over and over primary balance is achieved and the process of becoming a pitch has begun. Players need to know this drill has to eventually be perfect and therefore must be practiced over and over until they don't have to try so hard to be balanced. It can be done with lots of effort. Three seconds for this and each drill repeated four times. **The process is underway.**

Chapter 4
The Curl Drill

I use the Curl Drill to get pitchers of all ages to get their chest out over their knees when they pitch. This is an important part of the whole process to be able to pitch and throw strikes with velocity and accuracy. What will eventually happen is to teach pitchers to curl their glove to their arm pit. I want them to curl it with force while at the same time realize that if they aren't careful it could cause their front side to fly open. I spend time explaining that aspect of the pitch. "The ball goes where the shoulder leads." Before we attempt this drill I explain and demonstrate what I want them to do..........curl their glove to their arm pit with a sense of purpose while keeping their front shoulder pointed as long as possible at their target. I like to make this an early off season POE.......sometimes for the entire off season, every time they do drills with me. I stress that as their coach I want to hear as well as see the glove hit their arm pit. Again, it's necessary to be careful that they don't just curl the glove without being aware that they can cause the front shoulder to fly open. I also explain the reason to have them curl with some force. "For every action there is an equal and opposite reaction." Thank you Isaac Newton. If they curl the glove with force to their arm pit it thrusts their chest out over their knee which is what I hope to have all pitchers be able to do. This is the beginning of focusing all our energy of each pitch towards home plate. I don't want them back on their back foot when they throw. They have no power and thus no velocity. Stressing a closed front foot with the curl gives the pitcher as strong and powerful thrust towards home plate as they can have. I liken it to a boxer throwing a punch..........with an open front foot and punching off his back foot there isn't much of a punch being delivered. Okay, so what is the Curl Drill and how to do it?

Illustration 13

I first ask each student to place their heels on lines with their feet being stride length apart. **(Illustration 13)** They can achieve this by actually striding out as if they were pitching to judge their stride length.

Next I command, **"Ready, Ready."** This brings all players to the prayer position **Illustration 9**.

Illustration 14

I will then say **"Ready, Separate......Thumbs Down."** They separate their hands and I teach them at this time to look over their front shoulder at their target. I find it necessary when beginning this aspect of pitching to remind them that any time they separate their hands in the game of baseball not only do I like them to point their thumbs down but to also look over their front shoulder.....every time. **(Illustration 14)** It doesn't matter what position they play, every time they separate their hands they should automatically do these two things. So, in the drill they are stride width apart, in the prayer position and now have separated their hands.

Illustration 15

As they look over their front shoulder and their glove I give the next command…………."**Curl.**" At this point they pretend to throw their best fast ball, concentrating on first the curl (**Illustration 15**)…

Illustration 16

and second finishing their throw hand below their plant knee. **(Illustration 16)** I ask them to curl with enough force that I can hear the glove slapping against their chest and arm pit. I allow students to pretend to throw their best fast ball and once they finish below their plant knee they can immediately bounce back up. Be careful to not stand in front of a player using a heavy ball doing this drill as it could slip out of small or large hands. As with all drills, the curl drill is repeated four times each.

Chapter 5
The Heels Relations Drill

Again I will stress the necessity to repeat parts of drills learned previously in order to proceed fluidly into the next drill. Within the Heels Relation drill are aspects from the first two drills that will make this drill easier. The student must incorporate the glove curl and finish outside their plant knee with their throwing arm. Both are from the preceding drill. Now we are going to add to it. In the Heels Relation Drill I am stressing that every time a baseball is thrown the player needs to hit his lines. This drill is the beginning of doing this naturally. To achieve hitting our lines it must be stressed that the heels of both feet always line up. Thus the drill.

Illustration 17

Using a pitching tee or lines etched in the dirt or tape the pitcher first aligns both heels on a straight line. **(Illustration 17)** Feet remain stride length apart as in the Curl Drill.

Illustration 18

On the command **"Ready, Ready."** Pitchers go to the prayer position. Then on "Ready.....Pitch" they will curl the glove and throw their best fastball just as in the Curl Drill only now it becomes different. The pitcher stays down keeping his arm outside and below his plant knee. **(Illustration 18)**

Illustration 19 Illustration 20
Illustration 21 Illustration 22

As with all drills students hold this position for three seconds as I stress and check for five things:

1. Back heel pointing to the sky. **(Illustration 19,20)**
2. Slightly closed front foot. **(Illustration 19,21)**
3. A flat back. **(Illustration 19)**
4. Head up, eye on target. **(Illustration 19)**
5. Loose arm finish below plant knee. I call this the Elephant Trunk. **(Illustration 19,22)**

As a coach I want to see the pitcher concentrate on several things as he gets closer to throwing to a catcher. He can do all of this dry until he masters each drill. When doing the Heels Relations Drill I stress the importance of hitting our lines as the reason we line our heels up on a straight line prior to doing the drill. Next I stress that they need to repeat the five things I check quickly each time they repeat this drill. It's important that each item on this checklist be done properly. The closed front foot **(Illustration 21)** is necessary to have each pitch be delivered with maximum force. If the foot is open velocity is reduced and the possibility to fly open increases back foot with heel to the sky **(Illustration 20)** assists proper hip rotation getting the pitcher to focus on delivering the ball directly towards home plate and helps push the chest out over the knees. A flat back, not a ski slope or uphill climb **(Illustration 19)** helps a strong follow through and makes the defensive stance easier to attain. There will be more on that coming up. Head up, eyes on target **(Illustration 19)** helps the pitcher focus on his location.......which in my opinion for most pitchers even through high school is only the ability to throw the pitch across the plate. There may be the rare exceptional talent that can pitch to more exact spots........but wanting to keep it simple, the goal is to put the ball in play and the only way that is done is by throwing the ball across the plate consistently which is what happens when working on theses drills and not trying to be so perfect hitting spots. The last thing I check and insist on is a loose finish and complete follow through. In our drill I call it 'Elephant Trunk.' The finish is below the plant knee **(Illustration 19,22)** and should be loose. I want to see that follow through is attained and not stopped just after release. By having the kids swing their arm low and outside the plant knee until I stop them I can see follow through and they can feel it too. The Elephant Truck is not swung back and forth in front of the body.........that is a Grandfather Clock and proper arch of the pitch has not been successful.

Illustration 23

Illustration 24

Illustration 25

A right handed pitcher throwing a ball will have an arch that will start up and away from his right ear and finish crossing his body to finish below his left knee. **(Illustration 23,24,25)** Do this slowly many times just like doing the Prayer Position and separation to achieve what you want the pitcher to do. In the prayer position, separation you are looking for thumbs down to force the elbows up. In practicing the arch of the throw in slow motion the player will see where he needs to finish. One last note about the Elephant Trunk is to ask that the pitcher have a loose arm and loose shoulder and the coach should be able to see this clearly in this part of the drill. **On to my favorite drill...**

Chapter 6
Dot the Eye Drill (Secondary Balance)

One of my many constant sayings worth repeating is that in my opinion coaching pitchers for forty years is that a pitcher has to have balance. Primary Balance over the rubber is essential to any player wanting to pitch. Just as important is Secondary Balance which allows a pitcher to have complete follow through on every pitch as well as a consistent defensive stance once the pitch is delivered. The pitcher becomes the fifth infielder once the pitch is let go and must be able to field his position as any other infielder at this point. Pitchers who run off the mound or fall off to the plant foot side are not doing themselves any favors if they want to be the complete pitcher and team player. A pitcher must field come backers, bunts, swinging bunts, and cover first, make throws to second to start double plays and back up bases. If they are running off the mound none of these are done in a timely manner and could cause a big inning to occur. A pitcher is his own best friend defensively and this part of the game must be practiced and understood by the player wanting to be the best of the best. Secondary Balance puts the complete pitcher in position as an athlete to do his job defensively.

Once again stress that all aspects of previous drills are repeated as well doing any add on parts in the new drill is vital. I always stress that point prior to each new drill. **"Repeat Fundamentals"**……..is all I need to say before the **"Ready, Ready"** command. It's a useful trigger to warn the player not to "cheat the drill." If they are lazy and cheat any drill by not adequately repeating previous fundamental parts we go back to that previous drill…….or do Adler Push-ups. These are diamond push-ups to my very slow deliberate count. I do it in a fun way and never do more than a couple as

I remind them not to be lazy. It most often has the needed effect.

On the **"Ready, Ready"** command pitchers are in the exact same starting position as the Heels Relation Drill. We are just adding a couple important new parts.

Illustration 26

"Ready, Ready………Pitch." The pitcher as in both previous drills imitates his best fastball, glove curl and finish including the Elephant Trunk. The difference is he lifts his back leg "up and away." **(Illustration 26)** I challenge them to hold this Secondary Balance as I check for a closed front foot, flat back, head on target, and leg up and away and elephant trunk. After several seconds and challenges to hold it until Christmas or the Fourth of July I say **"Dot the Eye."** It takes some time to get pitchers to hold their balance and properly dot the eye.

Illustration 27

I tell them as a coach I want to see that they have complete control of this balance point and so when instructed to **"dot the eye"**……..I want them to lightly tap their toe as far behind them as they can. **(Illustration 27)** I ask that they learn to do this as if they were dotting the eye on a paper they write in school……ever so lightly then lift the leg back to the hold position. **(Illustration 26)**

Once they have raised the leg back up to Secondary Balance position I say **"Defensive Stance."** At this they set their leg down in what I call our 'butt down hands in front' defensive stance. **(Illustration 28)** I stress a soft landing as they set their raised foot down in the Defensive Stance. If they hop or jump into a defensive stance it is an extra movement that may throw off timing to get a jump to field their position. We are ready to put all the parts together.

Statue Drill Revisited

Now that we have an idea about Primary and Secondary Balances I can revisit this important drill. As I stated before I use this all season long in every time in pre practice or pregame when we play catch. As the team begins to wind down their warm up catch I will call out **"Statue Drill."** This alerts all pitchers regardless if they are pitching or not on that particular day to work on their craft of pitching. All other players if they are loose can jog in to the dugout. All pitchers however, know it's time to use their last several throw in a particular fashion.

Illustration 29   Illustration 30

They partner with another pitcher and throw using an exaggerated pause at both the Primary and Secondary Positions. I ask them to be like a statue. I ask them to come to a complete pause for one full second in the Primary Balance Position **(Illustration 29)** before continuing the pitch to pause again in the Secondary Balance Position **(Illustration 30)** for another complete second. I tease them that a pigeon should land on them if they do this drill properly. Once they execute four or five throws in this manner I call out **"Secondary Statue."** They now roll through a pitch only to hold just the Secondary Balance for a full second. I truly believe the more often a pitcher can work on his fundamentals the better he will be. By doing this drill every day before a game or pre practice the pitcher is getting in extra work. Doing some math if there are 100 hundred days in a season and pitchers do the Statue Drill every day they have worked on two specific fundamentals approximately 800-1000 extra times. That's working hard to be the best of the best.

Chapter 7
The Count Drill

I'm drill oriented and a coach who likes to build on fundamentals and work hard on little things. Therefore as we move through the process this next drill sums up all the parts as a whole and if done correctly moves the players close to being able to work on pitching to a catcher. The Count Drill allows me to control and check and recheck the player's fundamentals that we have been working on in all the other drills. I first remind students that we are working on a process and this gives me a chance to see if they are progressing. Sometimes in early lessons with young kids I hold off The Count Drill until I am certain all other fundamental drills have become natural. Once we get to this drill it's almost a reward to allow them to proceed. But, I still have control and will be coaching their fundamentals. If students are not able or willing to repeat even the smallest parts from previous drills we stop and revisit those fundamentals. If I have to I go back and repeat a previous drill.

Illustration 31

On the **"Ready, Ready"** command I ask the players to address the hitter **(Illustration 31)** with their feet close together. I like to use a pitch tee of scuffed lines in the dirt as we are going to be checking our lines on everything we do from this point forward.

You can use tape instead of scuffed lines in the dirt, but mark a T at the top and mark a longer line that extends from the bottom of the T straight for about three feet………..longer for taller pitchers. **(You can see the line out front in Illustration 33)**

Okay, here we go……….hang on there is much to this drill.

"Ready, Ready." Players are addressing the hitter and waiting for my count. **(Illustration 32)**

Illustration 33

- On **"One"** the pitcher looks down at his feet as he takes a very small momentum step. **(Illustration 33)** I like to have pitchers look down at their feet then on the next count look back up. I believe that if a pitcher stares at his target the whole time he will become too focused and end up aiming the ball. I like to break concentration for that one count then pick the target back up on the next count.

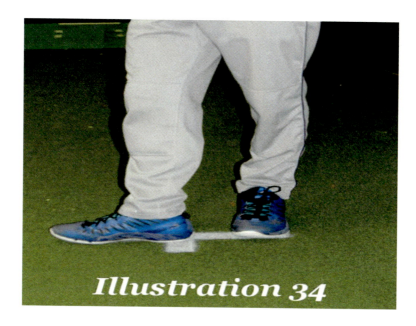

Illustration 34

- On **"Two"** the pitcher looks back up at his target and squares his back foot……..where have we seen this before? **(Illustration 34)**

Illustration 35

- On **"Three"** the pitcher goes to Primary Balance. **(Illustration 35)**

Illustration 36

- On **"Four"** the pitcher separates his hands, thumbs down and strides. **(Illustration 36)** I then say "Check your lines." This is where the T is useful. The pitchers look down to see if they have hit their lines. They adjust if they need to and I say **"look back up"** and we continue.

Illustration 37

- On **"Five"** the pitcher curls his glove **(Illustration 37)** and**....**

- Imitates his best fastball getting to the Secondary Balance position. **(Illustration 38)**

- On **"Six"** the pitcher Dots the Eye **(Illustration 39)** and raises the leg back up. **(Illustration 40)**

- On **"Seven"** the pitcher sets his back foot into a defensive stance. **(Illustration 41)**

- On **"Eight…….check your lines"** the pitcher checks to see if he has hit his lines. **(Illustration 42)**

As in all drills we do this one four times in a session. Doing this drill player and coach can't help but to see the importance of repeating previous fundamentals. We have just done a complete review of all drills in **The Count Drill** broken down into little parts of the whole. As a coach it is necessary not to rush to this drill or pass through it too quickly. As coach, I require a pause at each number to avoid this.

In Addition

I'm a proponent of an abbreviated windup, so **The Count Drill** is the first time we have a chance to address the issue of winding up or not. It's long been my theory to have my pitchers as "quiet" as they can when they pitch.

To this end I ask them to not wind up. I stress the hands stay in the middle of the chest until separation. **(Illustration 43)** I do this for a couple of reasons. I believe in keeping the ball and hands in the strike zone as long as possible. Once a pitcher begins an over the top wind up the ball leaves the strike zone. To this end I also ask that pitchers use a very small ready step when I count **"one"** .... small and straight back, not to a side, also to stay within the strike zone. Having pitchers keep the hands and feet in the strike zone as long as possible makes sense to me as a coach. Pitchers use both as reference points to begin their focus on moving everything towards the strike zone.

Chapter 8
The Pitch Drill

The last drill, also repeated four times I call the **Pitch Drill**. This is a chance to have the students imitate a real pitch. Firstly, though I take the opportunity to remind them of the mental aspect of pitching. As I ask them to address the hitter I remind them that the only thing in their mind should be **"Next Pitch Strike."** Often I will say **"Ready, Ready,"** our usual trigger to get them to the **Pray Position** and then ask a specific student if he remembers what our inning motto is.........."**Next Pitch Strike, Next Man Out**" borrowed from the best book I've read on pitching called <u>The Mental ABC's of Pitching by H.A. Dorfman</u>........a book all serious older pitchers should read. Now all students in the group are focused on beginning this last drill as they concentrate on what they should be thinking as they pitch. Again using humor I tell them I don't want them thinking 'of the girl with piggy tails sitting in the front row' or 'Uncle Charley spilling a chili cheese dog on his pants.' I want them to begin to understand the process to block out everything around them in order to concentrate on **"Next Pitch Strike."** I tell them the mind is their friend and a powerful tool when using positive thinking and imaging. See the strike in your mind.......think the strike in your mind.......block out everything else. If you are thinking of anything thing else throwing a strike is up for grabs. I believe the mind doesn't know what is real and what is not and therefore positive thoughts make positive results. I use paper plates on the wall to provide a reference point. With all students ready and focused I give some last quick encouragements.. "give him some attitude" or "you're better than he is." Now we're ready to throw an imitated pitch. **"Ready.........Pitch."** As the pitchers go through their fundamentals of throwing a pitch I calmly remind them "Go

Slow, Then Go Slower." This does not mean I want them to imitate a slow motion pitch. The opposite is true. I want them to throw their best imitated fast ball. However, I want them to remember constantly that a pitcher needs to go slow in order to gain balance and maintain their fundamentals. If they work too quickly it is very probable that there is no balance over the rubber and therefore he may have difficulty throwing strikes.

A coach positioned to the side of a pitcher can see if they are falling forward in the #3 position of the **Count Drill (Illustration 44)** instead of being rock solid balanced. As we repeat the drill, I ask a different student to tell me what he should be thinking............."**Next Pitch Strike, Next Man Out.**" This is also a calming exercise they can use during the game if they start to get themselves into trouble. Step off the mound. Deep breathe......"Repeat my fundamentals.......next pitch strike." During this drill I check to make sure each student is going slowly and has balance over the rubber. Placing me to the curl side of the pitcher is the best to view both these fundamentals. Upon completion of the imitated pitch I ask students to check their lines and if they did indeed throw a strike……..positive reinforcement.

I make sure that the students I have realize they can become their own pitching coach if they only realize that when they are not throwing strikes or things start to unravel they can remember to use Self-Talk to diagnose and calm themselves down. In all probability if they are not throwing strikes there are fundamental reasons why. More than likely they are rushing their delivery and also not gaining balance over the rubber. Both will go a long way to correct problems they are having. Using Self-Talk to slow themselves down and reminding themselves to repeat and trust their fundamentals can solve many issues on their own. Self-Talk can also calm a pitcher down to realize he may be just a double play ball or a pop up away from bailing themselves out of a problem. I tell the students when we are in lessons and throwing to catchers that if they are struggling on a particular day to step off our indoor mound and use Self-Talk to see if they can correct their issue. Often it's just a matter of balance and a reminder to trust and repeat their fundamental and then throw the pitch don't aim it. By slowing themselves down and using Self-Talk they begin to realize they are in charge of their own destiny. All they need do is execute those fundamentals I'm asking them to trust and repeat.

I'm also big on the mental approach to pitching and using mottos to encourage and motivate my students. I will include a glossary of sayings and terms I use at the end of this manual. Two I'm most fond of as we get to the Pitch Drill are a Game Day Motto and an Inning Motto. I ask the students to use Mental Practice the night before they know they are going to pitch whether it will be as a starter or reliever. I'm big on Triggers. I tell my players the night before games to use brushing their teeth as a trigger to begin Mental Practice for the game the next day. If they are to pitch I want them to think of our Game Day Motto and to lodge it firmly in their mental process..........Work Quickly, Throw Strikes and Change Speeds. I tell them if they do the first two their coaches and team mates will love them and if they do the third there is a very good chance they will be putting themselves in a position to win the game. This is not my motto. As I stated at the beginning of the manual I watched coaches and games of all kinds. Kept many notes and borrowed and experimented with many practices until I found those that worked successfully for me. Our Game Day Motto I borrowed from the Ray Miller who was in my opinion the best pitching coach the major leagues have had when he worked for the Baltimore Orioles in the 1970's. I loved his idea to Work Fast, Throw Strikes and Change Speeds. It seemed to simplify the mental approach to pitching especially in my region of the country with the cold springs. Even though this motto seems to be simple you have to get players to understand and buy into this approach by preaching it over and over. Then you must get them to use a trigger and mental practice when appropriate. As funny as these sounds I use brushing teeth the night before they know they will pitch as their trigger. I ask them to remember that when brush their teeth it should serve to remind them of their Game Motto. They then need to mental practice what it means to Work Fast, Throw Strikes and Change Speeds. They are getting mentally focused to execute our Game Motto.

As for our Inning Motto I tell the students that in a game situation every time they pick up or are handed the ball before they pitch in a particular inning they need to have tunnel vision and complete focus on their job to execute the Game Day Motto by throwing strikes first. Therefore our Inning Motto that they need to put into their mind prior to each pitch is "Next Pitch Strike, Next Man Out." I have borrowed this excellent advice from H. A. Dorfman's outstanding book on Pitching called <u>The Mental ABC's of Pitching</u>. He has so many key, important views on what a pitcher's mental approach should be that anyone serious about their craft should invest in his book. For my younger kids I ask them to just remember "Next Pitch Strike"……..older kids the whole saying, "Next Pitch Strike, Next Man Out." By blocking out everything around them and focusing on their Inning Motto they are giving themselves an excellent chance to throw those all-important strikes on a consistent basis.

In Summary

I don't pretend to be the highest authority on pitching or baseball for that matter but over the years I have been successful enough by using ideas from others wiser than I. Baseball is a passion of mine and as such I strive to teach it the proper way. I have always said that my priorities for my program might have differed from most but I believe that it has brought success and more importantly fun for my players. My program design is in this order of importance:

1. Pitching
2. Defense
3. Aggressive base running
4. Special offensive skills
5. Hitting

It took a few years to get kids to buy in to what I preached as a way to be successful but when it took hold it did just that. I want players to realize if we following this recipe we can play with anyone and give ourselves a chance to win any game. Over the years lesser talent teams have been competitive against even the most talented opponents. We give ourselves a chance late in the game because we throw strikes, pick up the ball and understand and practice the littlest details. But pitching is and will always be the most important part of the way I teach baseball. You have no chance to be competitive if your guy can't throw strikes and mix up speeds. But if he does, anything can happen. This is why we work so hard on pitching not only in season but in the off season and preseason. I will go into more details about this and holding runners in my future manuals.

It's sad to see kids not as in love with the game as I have always been. Kids in PE classes don't know the simplest rules of the game. They don't study the back of bubble gum cards to memorize stats as we did or trade them. I even knew who the first five members to Baseball's Hall of Fame were. I wonder how many can even get two of that group without using Google? It's time to rekindle the game deep into the souls of kids as it once was. By keeping the game simple and fun and helping them to play it the right way in my opinion is the starting point.

This is the greatest game in the world. Those who have the passion are bonded by the thrill of a well-played game. For me it's also the thrill of being able to teach the game to make this possible. I realize the way I learned and studied the game is a gift I give back with each lesson in hopes that America's game never loses its grip on those who dream to be the best of the best and play in The Bigs.

Good luck with your pitchers.

By the way……….Ruth, Cobb, Wagner, Mathewson and Johnson.

Be on the lookout for Coach Adler's next teaching manual coming in August 2014 that will stress drills for arm strengthening in the off season as well as a follow up to "How to Pitch" dealing with the importance of holding runners on base while working out of the stretch. Check his author page on Amazon for these and other books.

Glossary

Coach Adler Terms and Sayings:

"Address the Hitter"

The pitcher is looking in at the batter and his catcher prior to the pitch. Used verbally by coach in drills to focus students on the next task.

"Balance Over the Rubber"

This is the pitcher being in the primary balanced position while engaged with the rubber, not falling forward too soon as he pitches.

"The Ball Goes Where the Shoulder Leads"

To keep pitchers from 'flying open' this term is used to remind them to keep their front shoulder closed as long as possible as they throw.

"Brutal"

Endearing term used by Coach Adler to express displeasure with an assigned task.........as in "that was Brutal".....usually bringing a laugh from players within auditory range.

"Bulls-eyes"

When playing catch ask players to see a target on their partners' chest and to hit that target.

"Cadillac"

This term alerts catchers to relax as they catch pitchers in bullpen sessions after receiving several previous pitches in the ready position.

Count Drill

One of the six main pitching drills used as pitchers execute fundamentals learned.

Curl Drill

One of the six main pitching drills used to assist getting the chest out front over the knees.

Defensive Stance

This is the stance taken by the pitchers after releasing a pitch, necessary to be able to field his position at this moment.

"Don't Cheat the Drill"

Players who execute a drill in a lazy manner are cheating the drill.

Dot the Eye Drill

One of the six main pitching drills used to stress Secondary Balance.

Elephant Trunk

As pitchers finish a drill Elephant Trunk shows proper follow through as the arm swings free outside the plant leg.

"Flamingo"

This is a humorous reminder to not have a bent front leg in the Primary Balance Position.

"Flying Open"

This term refers to a pitchers front shoulder turning open too quickly and therefore pointing away from his target.

Game Motto

Pitchers must know and mental practice the motto to work fast, throw strikes and change speeds. (Ray Miller, Baltimore Orioles)

"Go Slow and Go Slower"

This useful reminder helps pitchers not rush his mechanics when in the wind-up.

"Grandfather Clock"

When in the finish position a player follows through across his body instead of outside his plant leg (Elephant Trunk).

Heels Relations Drill

One of the six main pitching drills used to help pitchers line up their heels as they throw.

"Hitting Our Lines"

Each time a players throws a baseball his heels should be aligned so that he is not flying open or throwing across his body.

Inning Motto

Pitchers block out all distractions and concentrate on "Next Pitch Strike, Next Man Out." (H.A. Dorfman, The ABC's of Mental Pitching.

"It's A Process"

My favorite motto used to help students learning to pitch take a long time with lot of effort.

Long Toss

If done correctly in the off season a useful drill to strength the arm. To be stressed in the next manual.

"Oh My Aching Crunch"

Endearing term one level of displeasure beyond "Brutal" bringing larger laughs from nearby players.......as in "Oh My Aching Crunch........that was Brutal."

Pitch Drill

The last of the six main pitching drills used to have pitchers demonstrate execution of all drills learned as they throw an imitated pitch.

"A Pitcher Must Have Balance"

Saying that is repeated often as a reminder to students that if they want to pitch they must demonstrate balance before anything else.

Pitching "T"

Either etched in the dirt or using tape a Pitching T is a model of a T at the top with a line useful to check hitting lines in drills.

Pray Position

Hands together as if praying prior to beginning each pitch drill.

Primary Balance Drill

The first of the six main pitching drills used to gain balance over the rubber.

"POE"

Point of Emphasis of a pitch session is to stress one fundamental over all others for that session.

"Ready Ready"

This is the trigger used by a coach to get all students in the Pray Position and ready to do a drill.

"Repeat Fundamentals"

Used most often with or replaced by "Trust Your Fundamentals" to remind pitchers that they must have confidence in the drills they have learned.

Secondary Balance

This is balance achieved as the ball is released which if executed correctly indicates fundamentals have been successful. Walking off or falling off the mound indicates no secondary balance which could lead to other issues.

Shuffle Change up Drill

Semi long tosses used with older pitchers to work on their change up grip and foot drag. To be stressed in the next manual.

Statue Drill

A two pronged drill that uses only a few throws every day for a pitcher to work on his primary and secondary balance points.

Thumbs Down

A trick taught that when separation occurs before throwing a pitch to turn thumbs down so both elbows are raised.

"Train"

Nickname used by Lancer players to identify Coach Adler.

Made in the USA
Lexington, KY
27 June 2018